AF609486

SHAPING THE DIGITAL FUTURE *with* EVERY LINE OF CODE

The Role of Engineers in Tomorrow's Technology

Omonzokpia George Okoidigun

Table Of Contents

FOREWORD

The digital age is no longer a distant future, it's the reality we live in today. Every facet of our lives, from the devices in our pockets to the systems that run global industries, is touched by the invisible yet profound force of code. As we witness rapid advancements in artificial intelligence, automation, and data science, it is clear that the architects of this digital world—engineers—hold a pivotal role in shaping the future. They are not merely builders of software or solvers of technical problems; they are the creators of tomorrow's society, influencing everything from how we communicate to how we address global challenges. The premise of this book, Shaping the Digital Future with Every Line of Code: The Role of Engineers in Tomorrow's Technology, is rooted in the understanding that engineers today wield a unique and powerful influence. With each decision they make, each solution they architect, and each line of code they write, they build the foundation for the future.

But with this influence comes responsibility—responsibility not just for technical accuracy or efficiency, but for ensuring that the technologies we create are ethical, inclusive, sustainable, and innovative. In the early days of computing, the role of the engineer was often viewed as largely technical. Coders were thought of as problem solvers, tasked with making systems work, optimizing performance, or enabling specific functions. Over time, however, the role of the engineer has expanded dramatically. Today, engineers are at the forefront of technological innovation, not just responding to existing problems but anticipating future needs and opportunities. They are creating the algorithms that power artificial intelligence, developing the software infrastructure for autonomous systems, and designing digital ecosystems that connect billions of people around the world. As engineers, we no longer have the luxury of working in isolation, disconnected from the broader societal implications of our work.

The technologies we develop impact economies, reshape industries, and influence the very nature of human interaction. For example, consider the way social media platforms, originally engineered as tools for communication, have transformed into some of the most powerful forces in global politics and culture. Or think of how autonomous vehicles, once seen as a futuristic concept, are now being developed with the potential to revolutionize transportation systems, logistics, and urban planning. The rapid pace of innovation demands that engineers think beyond the immediate technical challenges and consider the long-term consequences of their work. How will this new algorithm affect privacy and data security? How will a machine learning model ensure fairness and avoid bias? What role can engineers play in combating climate change through the design of energy-efficient software systems or green technologies? These are the questions that engineers must now grapple with, alongside the technical requirements of their work.

This book is a call to action for engineers everywhere—to not only embrace the vast potential of the digital revolution but to take an active role in shaping it for the better. It's about recognizing that the future of technology is in our hands, and with that power comes a moral imperative to create solutions that benefit all of society, not just a select few. Engineers must consider the ethical dimensions of their work, ensuring that the technologies we create are used for good, that they do not reinforce inequalities, and that they help build a sustainable and equitable future. Throughout this book, you will see how the role of the engineer has evolved from coder to innovator, from problem solver to strategic leader. You will explore the ways engineers are now tasked with building digital infrastructures as essential as the physical ones we rely on daily. You will read about how engineers are driving innovation in fields ranging from artificial intelligence and machine learning to renewable energy and healthcare.

The technologies they create will not only shape businesses and industries but will also define the way humans live, work, and interact for decades to come. As you engage with the content of this book, I encourage you to think about your own role as an engineer or technologist. Whether you are just starting your career or are a seasoned professional, you have the power to shape the future with every decision you make and every piece of code you write. Ask yourself not just how you can solve the technical problem in front of you, but how your work contributes to the larger goals of society. Are you building systems that empower people? Are you advancing technology in ways that will foster innovation, sustainability, and inclusion? Are you considering the ethical and societal implications of the tools you create? The future of technology is not inevitable; it is shaped by the decisions we make today. As engineers, we stand at the crossroads of innovation and responsibility.

The tools and technologies we create have the potential to transform the world in ways we can barely imagine—but only if we approach our work with vision, integrity, and purpose. I believe that Shaping the Digital Future with Every Line of Code will serve as both a guide and an inspiration for engineers seeking to understand the profound impact of their work. It provides not only a roadmap for mastering the technical challenges of the future but also a framework for thinking about the ethical and societal dimensions of engineering. Through the chapters of this book, you will see how the choices you make today as an engineer will define the world of tomorrow—and why those choices matter more than ever. So, let this book be a reminder of the incredible power you hold as an engineer. The future is built one line of code at a time, and with every keystroke, you have the opportunity to create a better, more equitable, and more sustainable world.

Let's get started. The future is waiting.

INTRODUCTION

Engineering the Future, One Line of Code at a Time

We live in a world where technology has permeated every aspect of our lives. From the smartphones in our pockets to the algorithms that recommend what we watch, listen to, or buy, technology shapes our daily experiences. It influences how businesses operate, how governments serve their citizens, and how we connect with each other across the globe. At the heart of this technological revolution are the engineers, the individuals who craft the software, build the hardware, and design the systems that power our digital world. Yet, the role of engineers is evolving rapidly. Today, engineers are more than just coders or technical problem solvers—they are the architects of the future. With each decision they make and each line of code they write, engineers have the power to shape the direction of entire industries, influence social outcomes, and solve some of the world's most pressing challenges. This transformation brings both incredible opportunities and immense responsibilities. This book, Shaping the Digital Future with Every Line of Code: The Role of Engineers in Tomorrow's Technology, aims to explore this pivotal moment in the history of engineering. It is a moment where the choices engineers make will have far-reaching consequences for the digital future we are collectively building. The book seeks to highlight the evolving role of engineers, the impact of their work on society, and the trends that will define the next era of technological innovation.

Engineers as Visionaries and Leaders

The digital age is often described as the Fourth Industrial Revolution, where advancements in artificial intelligence (AI), machine learning, cloud computing, and data science are transforming entire sectors and creating new ones. Engineers are the driving force behind these innovations. They are the ones who bring abstract ideas to life, translating concepts into code and algorithms that power groundbreaking applications and systems. But the role of the modern engineer goes beyond technical expertise. Engineers are now expected to be visionaries and leaders—professionals who understand not only how to build systems but also why those systems matter. Engineers must think about the broader implications of their work, including its economic, environmental, and ethical impacts. Consider the rise of autonomous vehicles. The engineers working on these technologies are not just solving technical problems like obstacle detection or route optimization, they are rethinking the future of transportation, urban mobility, and even labor markets. Autonomous vehicles will likely reduce traffic accidents and make transportation more efficient, but they also raise questions about job displacement for drivers, privacy concerns related to data collection, and the environmental impact of large-scale electric vehicle adoption.

Engineers are at the center of these debates, balancing technical innovation with societal outcomes.

The Power of Code: Crafting Tomorrow's Systems

It has been said that code is the new language of power. Just as industrial designers once shaped the world through mechanical engineering, today's engineers shape the world through software and algorithms. Every system that engineers create—from social media platforms to financial trading algorithms—has the potential to influence millions of lives. This power brings immense responsibility. The decisions made during the coding process are not just technical, they are ethical, social, and often political. Engineers must ask themselves questions like: Who will benefit from this technology? Who might be harmed? Is the system fair and inclusive? What are the long-term consequences of this solution? These are questions that every engineer should grapple with as they write the code that powers the next generation of technologies. Take artificial intelligence, for example. AI has the potential to revolutionize healthcare by providing faster, more accurate diagnoses and improving patient outcomes. However, the same AI systems could also perpetuate biases if they are trained on data that reflects existing social inequalities. An AI system designed to approve loan applications, for instance, could inadvertently discriminate against certain demographic groups if it relies on biased historical data. Engineers have a responsibility to ensure that the systems they design are ethical, fair, and transparent.

A New Era of Collaboration and Responsibility

One of the defining characteristics of modern engineering is the need for collaboration. Engineers no longer work in silos, focused only on coding or technical development. Today, successful engineers must collaborate across disciplines, working alongside business leaders, product managers, data scientists, designers, and policymakers to ensure that the technology they build serves the broader needs of society. In this new era, engineering decisions are often intertwined with business strategy. Engineers are expected to understand the business context in which they are working—whether it's optimizing revenue streams for a SaaS platform, enhancing user engagement for a mobile app, or designing scalable infrastructure for a global enterprise. Engineers must also work closely with other departments to ensure that their technical solutions align with the company's strategic goals and meet user needs. This collaborative approach extends beyond the boundaries of individual companies. Open-source software, for instance, has revolutionized the way engineers work. Open-source projects are built by communities of engineers from around the world, each contributing their expertise to create systems that are used by millions. These projects exemplify the idea that the future of technology is a shared effort, built by a global community of engineers working toward common goals. Alongside collaboration, there is a growing recognition of engineers' responsibility to society. As technology increasingly shapes our economies, politics, and cultures, engineers are being called upon to address complex issues like data privacy, cybersecurity, and the ethical use of AI. The systems engineers build must protect user rights, ensure fairness, and guard against misuse. Engineers are also at the forefront of addressing global challenges like climate change, using technology to create more sustainable systems that reduce energy consumption, minimize waste, and promote environmental stewardship.

Preparing for the Future

As we look ahead, the role of engineers will continue to evolve. Engineers of the future will need to be adaptable, continuously learning new skills and embracing emerging technologies. They will need to be both technical experts and strategic thinkers, able to balance the demands of innovation with the need for ethical and responsible development. In the coming years, we will see new technologies emerge that will redefine industries, from quantum computing and blockchain to advanced robotics and biotechnology. Each of these technologies will present new opportunities and new challenges for engineers. The engineers who thrive in this future will be those who are not only proficient in the latest coding languages or development frameworks but also those who are willing to ask the hard questions, think creatively, and lead with a sense of purpose.

What You Will Learn in This Book

This book is designed to guide engineers through the complexities of shaping tomorrow's technology. In the chapters that follow, we will explore the evolving role of engineers and the critical part they play in shaping the digital future. We will look at how engineers can:

Drive innovation and create disruptive technologies that change industries.

- Build ethical, responsible, and inclusive systems that benefit society as a whole.
- Navigate the challenges of scaling complex software systems in a global, interconnected world.
- Collaborate with cross-functional teams to align technical development with business strategy.
- Leverage emerging technologies like AI, blockchain, and quantum computing create solutions for tomorrow's challenges.
- Contribute to sustainability and use engineering to tackle climate change and other global issues.

The journey of an engineer is not just about mastering technology—it's about using that mastery to shape the world in meaningful ways. Whether you're an experienced engineer or just starting out, this book will offer insights, inspiration, and practical guidance for navigating the challenges and opportunities of the digital future.

The Time is Now

The future is not something that happens to us; it is something we create. As engineers, we are uniquely positioned to shape that future, one line of code at a time. This book is a call to action for engineers everywhere to embrace their role as leaders, innovators, and problem solvers, not just in technology but in society at large. In the following pages, you will explore how every decision, every system, and every algorithm you build has the potential to influence the future. The question is: What kind of future do you want to create?

CHAPTER 1

The Evolution of Software Engineering

Software engineering has come a long way since the early days of computing, when computers were room-sized machines operated by a handful of pioneers. In just a few decades, software engineering has transformed from a niche discipline into the backbone of the digital world, shaping industries, economies, and societies in unprecedented ways. Engineers today build systems that touch nearly every aspect of our lives, from the algorithms that suggest our next favorite song to the autonomous vehicles that navigate busy streets. Yet, this transformation didn't happen overnight—it was the result of continuous evolution, driven by technological breakthroughs, shifting industry needs, and the ingenuity of engineers. This chapter explores the evolution of software engineering, tracing its roots from the early days of programming to its current role as the foundation of modern technology. We will look at key milestones in software development, the challenges engineers have faced along the way, and how the role of the engineer has expanded far beyond coding to become a critical strategic force in shaping the future.

Early Days of Software Development: From Punch Cards to the Birth of Programming

The history of software engineering began with the creation of the first computers in the mid-20th century. Early computing machines, such as ENIAC and UNIVAC, were massive, room-sized devices used primarily for scientific calculations and military applications. Programming these machines was laborious, requiring engineers to manually input instructions using punch cards or switches. The process was slow, error-prone, and highly specialized—far removed from the intuitive development environments we have today. In the 1950s, the need for more sophisticated and efficient ways to program computers led to the development of the first high-level programming languages. FORTRAN (Formula Translation) was introduced in 1957 by IBM, marking a major breakthrough in software development. FORTRAN allowed engineers to write programs using more human-readable syntax, which made programming more accessible and less dependent on machine-specific code. Following FORTRAN, COBOL (Common Business-Oriented Language) was created to support business data processing, and it became widely used in industries such as banking and government. Despite these advances, software development remained a large manual process, with each program tailored to specific machines and tasks. There was little focus on reusability, scalability, or formalized engineering principles. As computing power grew and the demand for software increased, the limitations of these early approaches became more apparent. Software projects often ran over budget, were delivered late, and, in many cases, failed to meet expectations. The growing complexity of software systems led to the realization that coding alone was not enough—there needed to be a more structured, disciplined approach to building software. This set the stage for the formalization of software engineering as a distinct field.

The Birth of Software Engineering as a Discipline

The term "software engineering" was coined in 1968 during a conference organized by NATO, in response to what was described as the "software crisis." This crisis referred to the increasing difficulty of managing large, complex software projects, which often led to cost overruns, missed deadlines, and unreliable software. Engineers and computer scientists recognized that the ad hoc methods of programming were not sufficient to meet the growing demands of industry and society. The goal of software engineering was to apply principles from traditional engineering disciplines—such as standardization, modularity, and rigorous testing—to the development of software. This shift marked the beginning of a more structured, systematic approach to building software systems. The focus moved from merely writing code to designing robust architectures, managing development processes, and ensuring quality through testing and validation. Key concepts such as modularity, abstraction, and software reuse began to gain prominence. These ideas allowed engineers to break down complex systems into smaller, more manageable components, making it easier to develop, test, and maintain software over time. The rise of structured programming, championed by languages like Pascal and C, emphasized the importance of clear, logical code structures and formalized the concept of procedures and functions. The software crisis also led to the development of formal methodologies for managing software projects. Early methods like the Waterfall Model, introduced in the 1970s, provided a linear framework for software development, moving from requirements gathering to design, implementation, testing, and maintenance in sequential stages. While the Waterfall Model helped bring order to chaotic software projects, its rigid structure made it difficult to accommodate changes once development was underway—a limitation that would lead to the evolution of more flexible approaches in the future.

The Rise of Object-Oriented Programming and Agile Methodologies

The 1980s and 1990s saw significant advancements in software engineering, driven by the increasing complexity of software systems and the need for more adaptable development methodologies. One of the most transformative innovations of this era was the rise of object-oriented programming (OOP). Languages like C++, Java, and Smalltalk introduced the concept of objects—self-contained units of code that encapsulate both data and behavior. Object-oriented programming offered a more intuitive way to model real-world systems, making it easier to manage complexity and reuse code. Object-oriented programming became the foundation for many modern software systems, allowing engineers to build more modular, scalable, and maintainable software. OOP also paved the way for the development of design patterns—standardized solutions to common programming problems. Design patterns, popularized by the book Design Patterns: Elements of Reusable Object-Oriented Software (also known as the "Gang of Four" book), provided engineers with a toolkit for solving common design challenges, further formalizing the craft of software development. However, as software projects continued to grow in size and scope, the limitations of the Waterfall Model became increasingly apparent. The rigid, linear approach to development did not allow for the iterative nature of modern software projects, where requirements often evolve during the development process. In response, the Agile Manifesto was introduced in 2001, marking a radical shift in how the software was built. Agile methodologies, such as Scrum and Kanban, emphasized collaboration, flexibility, and iterative development. Rather than defining all project requirements upfront, Agile teams work in short cycles, called sprints, to deliver incremental updates to the software. This approach allows for continuous feedback, faster delivery of value, and the ability to adapt to changing requirements. Agile has since become the dominant methodology for software development, empowering engineers to work more closely with stakeholders and create software that meets evolving user needs.

The Open-Source Revolution

While Agile methodologies reshaped the way teams worked internally, another major shift was happening in the broader software community: the rise of open-source software. Open-source projects, such as Linux, Apache, and MySQL, showed the world that large-scale, high-quality software could be developed collaboratively by engineers across the globe, without the need for proprietary ownership. The open-source movement transformed the software landscape, making powerful tools and libraries available to developers for free. This democratization of technology accelerated innovation, allowing engineers to build on the work of others and focus on solving new problems rather than reinventing the wheel. Open-source development also introduced new models of collaboration, where engineers from different companies, countries, and backgrounds could contribute to shared projects. Today, open-source software forms the foundation of much of the internet and cloud infrastructure. Companies like Google, Facebook, and Microsoft contribute extensively to open-source communities, recognizing that collaboration is key to driving technological progress. Engineers who participate in open-source projects not only gain valuable skills but also help shape the future of software by contributing to tools that are used by millions worldwide.

The Modern Engineer: Solving Complex, Global Problems

As we enter the 21st century, the role of the engineer has expanded beyond writing code to solving some of the most complex and pressing challenges facing society. From designing systems that handle billions of transactions per second to building AI algorithms that can diagnose diseases or predict climate patterns, engineers are at the forefront of innovation. The rise of cloud computing, microservices, and DevOps practices has revolutionized how software is built, deployed, and maintained at scale. Engineers are now responsible for designing systems that can handle global demand, ensuring uptime and reliability across distributed networks. The expectation is no longer just to deliver functional software but to ensure that software is scalable, secure, and resilient in an increasingly interconnected world. In addition, engineers are increasingly called upon to consider the ethical implications of their work. With the rise of AI and machine learning, concerns about bias, privacy, and accountability have come to the forefront. Engineers must not only be skilled in technical development but also in understanding the societal impacts of the technologies they create. The work of engineers now intersects with fields such as ethics, law, and public policy, requiring a multidisciplinary approach to technology development.

The evolution of software engineering has been marked by continuous innovation, from the early days of punch cards to the modern era of cloud-native applications and AI-driven systems. Engineers have played a central role in this evolution, driving technological progress and shaping the digital world we live in today. However, the journey is far from over. As the world becomes more connected and reliant on digital systems, the role of engineers will continue to expand. The next generation of engineers will be tasked with solving problems on a global scale, from addressing climate change to ensuring data privacy in an age of ubiquitous surveillance. In the chapters that follow, we will explore how engineers can continue to shape the future through their work, embracing new technologies, ethical frameworks, and collaborative approaches to build a digital world that benefits everyone. Whether you're a seasoned engineer or just starting your career, the role you play in this future is critical—and the possibilities are limitless.

CHAPTER 2

The Modern Engineer: More Than a Coder

The image of the lone coder, hunched over a keyboard, surrounded by empty coffee cups, working late into the night to solve complex problems, is an enduring one in popular culture. While coding remains an essential skill for engineers, the role of the modern engineer has evolved far beyond that of a solitary programmer. In today's world, engineers are not just technical specialists, they are innovators, leaders, collaborators, and strategists. The modern engineer operates at the intersection of technology, business, and society. They are tasked not only with developing functional systems but also with understanding user needs, driving business value, and ensuring that the solutions they create are ethical and inclusive. This chapter explores the many facets of the modern engineer's role and highlights how today's engineers are transforming industries, influencing business strategy, and solving global challenges.

Engineers as Problem Solvers and Innovators

At its core, engineering is about solving problems. Engineers are trained to approach problems methodically, breaking them down into smaller, more manageable components, and designing solutions that are efficient, scalable, and reliable. However, the scope of the problems engineers are expected to solve has expanded significantly over time. In the past, engineers were primarily tasked with solving technical problems, how to make a system run more efficiently, how to improve performance, or how to scale an application to handle more users. While these remain important aspects of the job, the problems engineers face today are often more complex and multifaceted, involving not just technical challenges but also considerations of user experience, business strategy, and societal impact. For example, an engineer working at a tech company might be tasked with developing an e-commerce platform. While the technical challenge might involve designing a scalable architecture, the engineer must also consider how the platform will affect the company's revenue, how it will deliver value to customers, and how it will differentiate the business from competitors.

Engineers today are expected to think holistically, taking into account both the technical and non-technical aspects of the problems they are solving. This shift from purely technical problem solving to innovation has transformed the role of the engineer. Engineers are now seen as key drivers of innovation within their organizations, responsible for developing new products, services, and systems that can disrupt industries and create new business opportunities. This requires not only technical expertise but also creativity, vision, and an understanding of market trends. Consider the development of the smartphone. While the technical challenge of designing a mobile computing device was significant, the engineers behind the first smartphones were also innovators, reimagining how people would communicate, work, and entertain themselves in a world where everyone has a powerful computer in their pocket. The success of the smartphone wasn't just about solving technical problems, it was about seeing the potential for a device that would change the way we live.

Engineers as Strategic Thinkers

In today's business environment, technology is often at the core of strategic decision-making. Companies across all industries—whether in retail, finance, healthcare, or entertainment—rely on digital systems to drive revenue, optimize operations, and engage with customers. As a result, engineers have become essential contributors to business strategy, working closely with leadership to ensure that technology solutions are aligned with the company's broader goals. The modern engineer must be able to bridge the gap between technology and business, understanding both the technical requirements of a project and its strategic importance. This requires a deep understanding of the company's objectives, the competitive landscape, and the needs of customers. Engineers who can think strategically are better positioned to develop solutions that deliver real business value and drive long-term success. For example, an engineer at a logistics company might be tasked with developing a route optimization algorithm to improve delivery efficiency. While the technical challenge is significantly building an algorithm that can calculate the most efficient routes for thousands of deliveries each day, the engineer must also consider the broader business implications. How will the algorithm affect operational costs? How will it improve customer satisfaction by reducing delivery times? How can the solution scale as the company expands into new markets? By thinking strategically, the engineer can design a solution that not only solves the technical problem but also supports the company's growth and profitability. This alignment between engineering and business strategy is critical in today's competitive environment, where technology is often the key differentiator between success and failure.

Engineers as Collaborators

Gone are the days when engineers worked in isolation, coding away in the back office. Today's engineers operate in highly collaborative environments, working alongside product managers, designers, marketers, and business leaders to develop solutions that meet the needs of users and the goals of the company. Collaboration is particularly important in the development of complex systems, where different teams must work together to ensure that all aspects of the project are aligned. Engineers must collaborate with product managers to understand user needs and translate those needs into technical requirements. They must work with designers to ensure that the user interface is intuitive and user-friendly. They must coordinate with marketing and sales teams to understand how the product will be positioned in the market and how its features will be communicated to customers. Collaboration is also essential in an increasingly globalized world, where teams are often distributed across different time zones and locations. Engineers must be able to communicate effectively, share knowledge, and work together to solve problems, even when they are not physically in the same place. Tools like Slack, GitHub, and Jira have become essential for enabling remote collaboration, allowing engineers to track progress, share code, and discuss issues in real-time. One of the most significant trends in engineering collaboration is the rise of cross-functional teams—teams that bring together individuals from different disciplines to work on a common project. In a cross-functional team, engineers work alongside product managers, data scientists, designers, and marketers, each contributing their unique expertise to the development process. This collaborative approach ensures that all aspects of the project are considered, from technical feasibility to user experience to business impact.

For example, in the development of a new mobile app, a cross-functional team might include:

Engineers, who are responsible for building the app's backend and frontend systems.

Product managers, who define the app's features and ensure that they align with user's needs and business goals.

Designers, who create the app's user interface and ensure that it is visually appealing and easy to use.

Data scientists, who analyze user behavior and provide insights that inform product development.

Marketers, who plan how the app will be promoted and how its value proposition will be communicated to users.

Engineers as Lifelong Learners

In a field as dynamic as software engineering, continuous learning is essential. New programming languages, frameworks, and tools are constantly being introduced, and engineers must stay up to date with the latest developments to remain effective in their roles. However, the need for continuous learning goes beyond technical skills. Engineers must also stay informed about emerging trends in business, user experience, and ethics to ensure that their work remains relevant and impactful. This requires a commitment to lifelong learning, not only through formal education but also through on-the-job experience, reading, networking, and participation in industry events. For example, an engineer working on cloud infrastructure might need to learn about new technologies like serverless computing or containerization to improve the scalability and efficiency of their systems. At the same time, they might also need to stay informed about trends in data privacy and security to ensure that their systems comply with regulations like the General Data Protection Regulation (GDPR).

Lifelong learning is not just a necessity, it is also an opportunity. Engineers who embrace a growth mindset and actively seek out new knowledge are better positioned to innovate, lead, and shape the future of their industry. The role of the modern engineer is multifaceted, encompassing far more than writing code. Today's engineers are problem solvers, innovators, strategic thinkers, collaborators, ethical stewards, and lifelong learners. They are responsible for building the systems that power our digital world, but they are also tasked with ensuring that those systems deliver value to users, support business goals, and contribute to a better society. In the next chapter, we will explore how engineers are building the digital infrastructure of tomorrow, creating systems that are as critical to modern life as physical infrastructures like roads and power grids. But as we move forward, it's important to recognize that engineers are not just builders, they are shapers of the future, and their work will define the world for generations to come.

CHAPTER 3

Code as Infrastructure: Building Tomorrow's Digital Cities

In the past, infrastructure referred to the physical systems that enabled societies to function: roads, bridges, railways, power grids, and water systems. These systems, built by civil engineers, provided the foundational framework upon which modern life was constructed. Today, however, a new type of infrastructure has emerged—one that is just as critical to the functioning of our global economy and everyday lives: digital infrastructure. Digital infrastructure consists of the systems, platforms, and software that power everything from communication networks and cloud services to financial transactions and global logistics. It is no longer possible to imagine a world without the invisible frameworks of code that keep our digital cities running. And just as civil engineers once built the physical infrastructure of roads and bridges, software engineers are now tasked with building the digital highways of the future. This chapter explores the concept of code as infrastructure, examining how engineers are creating resilient, scalable, and secure digital systems that are as essential as physical infrastructure. We will look at the key components of digital infrastructure, the challenges of building systems at scale, and the ways in which engineers are ensuring that the digital cities of tomorrow are efficient, accessible, and sustainable.

The Rise of Digital Infrastructure

At the turn of the 21st century, the idea of software as infrastructure was still in its infancy. The internet was growing rapidly, but it was not yet the essential component of daily life that it has become today. Back then, businesses still operated with physical storefronts, employees worked in local offices, and communication was primarily conducted via phone or fax. Digital systems were seen as valuable but optional enhancements to existing physical infrastructure. However, as the internet grew, so too did the reliance on digital systems. Today, digital infrastructure has become indispensable. Without it, many of the systems we rely on—banking, transportation, healthcare, education, and commerce—would grind to a halt. Every online purchase, every streamed movie, every virtual meeting, and every automated supply chain transaction depends on the invisible infrastructure of code that keeps the digital world running. Cloud Computing is perhaps the most important example of modern digital infrastructure. Companies like Amazon Web Services (AWS), Microsoft Azure, and Google Cloud provide the computational power, storage, and network capacity that businesses of all sizes need to operate. Rather than building their own data centers, companies can now leverage the vast resources of the cloud, allowing them to scale their operations quickly and efficiently. Cloud platforms have become the backbone of digital infrastructure, enabling everything from e-commerce websites to streaming platforms to function without interruption.

But cloud computing is just one part of the broader digital infrastructure landscape. Other critical components include:

Communication Networks: The fiber-optic cables, satellites, and cellular towers that connect billions of devices worldwide. Without fast and reliable internet connections, digital infrastructure would be unusable.

Data Centers: The physical buildings that house the servers and storage systems powering cloud computing, web hosting, and other digital services.

Cybersecurity Systems: The firewalls, encryption algorithms, and threat detection systems that protect data and systems from cyberattacks.

Payment Gateways: The digital platforms that process trillions of dollars in financial transactions, ensuring that commerce can flow smoothly across borders and industries.

This digital infrastructure is not only essential for businesses, but it also underpins the functioning of governments, educational institutions, and healthcare systems. Governments use digital systems to manage public services, hospitals rely on electronic health records and telemedicine platforms, and schools use online learning tools to educate students remotely. Without a robust digital infrastructure, modern life as we know it would be impossible.

Building for Scale: The Engineer's Challenge

One of the defining features of digital infrastructure is its ability to scale. Unlike physical infrastructure, which is constrained by geography and physical resources, digital infrastructure can scale up to meet the needs of billions of users, regardless of their location. This ability to scale is both a tremendous advantage and a significant challenge for engineers. Consider a global platform like YouTube, which serves billions of video viewers every day. The platform needs to handle vast amounts of data, process videos in multiple formats, and deliver seamless viewing experiences to users around the world. To achieve this, YouTube's engineers must design systems that are not only efficient and reliable but also capable of scaling to meet the ever-growing demand for video content. Similar challenges exist for other global platforms like Facebook, Amazon, and Netflix, where scalability is key to success. Building scalable systems requires engineers to think beyond the immediate needs of their users and plan for future growth. This involves designing architectures that can handle increased traffic, optimizing algorithms to ensure efficiency, and ensuring that systems remain reliable even as they scale to global proportions.

Engineers must also consider factors like data replication, fault tolerance, and load balancing to ensure that systems continue to function even when parts of the infrastructure fail. Distributed Systems are a critical component of scalable digital infrastructure. In a distributed system, computing resources are spread across multiple locations, allowing for parallel processing and redundancy. This ensures that if one part of the system goes down, the other parts can continue to function. For example, Netflix uses a distributed system architecture to deliver streaming content to millions of users simultaneously. By replicating data across multiple servers and using sophisticated load-balancing algorithms, Netflix ensures that users can stream content without interruption, even if one server experiences issues. While scalability is a technical challenge, it also requires a deep understanding of business needs. Engineers must work closely with business leaders to understand growth projections, user behavior, and market trends. This collaboration ensures that the systems engineers build are not only technically sound but also aligned with the company's long-term goals.

Building Resilience: Ensuring Uptime and Security

In addition to scalability, resilience is another critical requirement for digital infrastructure. In today's 24/7 digital world, systems must remain online and functional at all times. Even a brief outage can lead to significant financial losses, damage to reputation, and disruptions to essential services. For example, when Amazon Web Services experienced a major outage in 2020, it affected thousands of businesses that rely on AWS for their digital operations, highlighting the importance of resilience in cloud computing. Engineers must design systems that can recover quickly from failures and continue to operate under adverse conditions. This involves implementing redundancy, where multiple copies of critical data and systems are maintained in different locations. In the event of a failure, the system can switch to a backup copy without users noticing any disruption. For example, Google maintains multiple data centers around the world, each capable of taking over if another data center goes offline. This level of redundancy ensures that Google's services, such as Gmail and Google Search, remain available even in the event of a major infrastructure failure.

Engineers at Google have also developed automated systems to monitor the health of their infrastructure and automatically route traffic to healthy servers when an issue is detected. Cybersecurity is another key aspect of resilience. As digital infrastructure becomes more critical to daily life, it also becomes a target for cyberattacks. Engineers must implement robust security measures to protect systems from threats like malware, ransomware, and denial-of-service attacks. This includes encrypting sensitive data, building secure authentication systems, and regularly updating software to patch vulnerabilities. One of the most significant challenges in cybersecurity is the constant evolution of threats. Engineers must stay ahead of cybercriminals by developing adaptive security systems that can detect and respond to new threats in real-time. For example, many companies now use AI-powered cybersecurity systems that analyze network traffic for suspicious activity and automatically take action to prevent an attack before it causes damage.

Digital Infrastructure as a Public Good: The Role of Engineers

As digital infrastructure becomes as essential as electricity or clean water, there is a growing recognition that it should be treated as a public good—something that is accessible to everyone, regardless of their geographic location or socioeconomic status. Engineers play a crucial role in ensuring that digital infrastructure is built in a way that promotes accessibility, inclusivity, and equity. In many parts of the world, access to digital infrastructure is still limited, particularly in rural areas and developing countries. Engineers are working to bridge this digital divide by developing technologies that extend internet access to underserved communities. For example, Google's Project Loon uses high-altitude balloons to deliver internet access to remote areas, while SpaceX's Starlink project aims to provide global internet coverage through a network of low-Earth orbit satellites. Engineers are also developing technologies that make digital infrastructure more accessible to people with disabilities. For example, engineers working on web development standards have created tools and frameworks that ensure websites are compatible with screen readers and other assistive technologies.

These efforts are critical in ensuring that the digital cities of tomorrow are inclusive and accessible to everyone. Sustainability is another important consideration in the development of digital infrastructure. Data centers, which power much of the world's digital systems, consume vast amounts of electricity, contributing to carbon emissions. Engineers are working to develop more energy-efficient data centers and reduce the environmental impact of digital infrastructure. For example, Microsoft has committed to powering its data centers with 100% renewable energy by 2025, and engineers at Google have developed AI algorithms that optimize data center cooling, reducing energy consumption.

Smart Cities and the Future of Urban Infrastructure

One of the most exciting applications of digital infrastructure is the development of smart cities—urban areas that use digital technologies to improve the efficiency of services, reduce environmental impact, and enhance the quality of life for residents. Engineers play a central role in designing and implementing the digital infrastructure that powers smart cities, from IoT (Internet of Things) networks to intelligent transportation systems. For example, Singapore has become a global leader in smart city development, using data and digital technologies to manage everything from traffic flow to energy consumption. Engineers have developed a network of sensors and cameras that collect real-time data on traffic patterns, which is then used to optimize traffic light timings and reduce congestion. Smart meters installed in buildings monitor energy usage, allowing residents to track and reduce their energy consumption. These technologies, combined with advanced data analytics, have transformed Singapore into one of the most efficient and sustainable cities in the world.

As cities continue to grow, smart city technologies will play an increasingly important role in managing urban infrastructure. Engineers will be tasked with developing systems that can handle the complexity of modern cities, from managing transportation networks to optimizing energy grids. These systems will need to be scalable, resilient, and secure, ensuring that the digital cities of tomorrow are efficient, sustainable, and livable. Digital infrastructure has become the foundation of modern life, enabling everything from online communication and commerce to healthcare and public services. Engineers are the architects of this infrastructure, responsible for building systems that are scalable, resilient, and secure. As digital infrastructure becomes more critical to society, engineers must also consider issues of accessibility, sustainability, and inclusivity, ensuring that the benefits of digital infrastructure are shared by all. In the chapters to come, we will explore the ethical responsibilities of engineers, the challenges of building scalable systems, and the ways in which engineers can drive innovation and create a more sustainable future. But as we move forward, it's important to recognize that the work of engineers today is laying the foundation for the digital cities of tomorrow—cities where code is the infrastructure that keeps everything running.

CHAPTER 4

Coding for Scale: Managing Complexity in the Digital Age

As digital systems become the foundation of global businesses and essential services, engineers face the increasingly complex challenge of building software that can scale to meet vast demands. Whether it's an e-commerce platform that processes millions of transactions daily, a social media site with billions of users, or an autonomous vehicle fleet generating terabytes of data every second, the ability to scale is critical to success. But scaling a system isn't just about adding more servers or bandwidth; it requires careful design, robust architectures, and a deep understanding of both software and infrastructure. This chapter explores the art and science of coding for scale, delving into the principles, challenges, and best practices engineers must master to build systems that can grow without sacrificing performance, security, or reliability. We'll explore case studies from industry giants like Amazon, Netflix, and Google to understand how they've solved scalability challenges, and we'll look at the key strategies engineers can adopt to manage complexity in the digital age.

The Challenge of Scale

One of the defining characteristics of modern digital systems is their ability to serve a global audience. Unlike traditional physical systems, which are often constrained by geographic limitations, digital systems can grow quickly and reach users anywhere in the world. This scalability is both an opportunity and a challenge. At small scales, many software systems are easy to manage. A small e-commerce website, for example, might handle a few hundred transactions a day with little strain. But as that site grows, the load on its infrastructure increases exponentially. Suddenly, it must process millions of transactions, store terabytes of customer data, and handle complex pricing algorithms—all while ensuring a smooth user experience. The key challenge for engineers is to ensure that the system grows seamlessly without becoming slow, error-prone, or insecure.

Scalability can be broken down into two main types:

Vertical Scaling: Also known as scaling up, this involves increasing the capacity of a single server by adding more resources (CPU, memory, etc.).

Horizontal Scaling: Also known as scaling out, this involves adding more machines to handle the increased load, distributing tasks across multiple servers.

While vertical scaling can be useful for small systems, horizontal scaling is generally preferred for large-scale systems because it allows for greater flexibility and redundancy. However, designing systems that can scale horizontally presents significant architectural challenges, requiring engineers to think about data distribution, load balancing, and fault tolerance.

Building for Scale: Principles of Scalability

Building scalable systems requires engineers to adopt certain design principles that ensure a system can handle growth without degradation in performance. Let's explore some of the key principles of building for scale: Distributed Systems At the heart of most large-scale systems is the concept of distributed computing. In a distributed system, tasks are spread across multiple machines, allowing the system to process larger amounts of data and handle more users simultaneously.

1. Distributed Systems: provide scalability and fault tolerance by ensuring that the failure of a single machine doesn't bring down the entire system. One of the challenges of distributed systems is ensuring consistency and availability across all nodes. This is where the CAP Theorem comes into play, which states that in any distributed system, you can only achieve two of the following three properties:

Consistency: All nodes see the same data at the same time.

Availability: Every request receives a response, whether successful or failed.

Partition Tolerance: The system continues to operate even if communication between some nodes is lost.

Engineers must make trade-offs based on the requirements of the system. For example, financial systems often prioritize consistency, while social media platforms might prioritize availability.

2. Microservices Architecture: As systems grow in complexity, the traditional monolithic architecture, where all components of a system are tightly coupled, becomes harder to scale. A more scalable approach is the microservices architecture, where a system is broken down into independent services that communicate through APIs. Each microservice is responsible for a specific function (e.g., payment processing, user authentication) and can be scaled independently of the others. This modularity allows teams to develop, deploy, and scale different parts of the system without affecting the entire application. For instance, if the payment system is experiencing high demand, engineers can scale only that microservice rather than the entire application. Companies like Netflix and Amazon have embraced microservices architectures to scale their services and handle millions of users and transactions simultaneously. The use of microservices has allowed them to build systems that are not only scalable but also flexible and easier to maintain.

3. Load Balancing: One of the most important components of scaling a system is load balancing, which ensures that incoming requests are distributed evenly across multiple servers. Load balancing prevents any single server from becoming overwhelmed by traffic, which could cause performance degradation or outages. Round-robin, least connections, and IP hash are common algorithms used for load balancing. Additionally, modern systems often use smart load balancers that can dynamically adjust traffic distribution based on real-time server performance and health. For example, when Amazon experiences traffic spikes during events like Prime Day, its load balancers distribute traffic across hundreds of servers, ensuring that the website remains responsive even under extreme load.

4. Caching: Caching is a crucial technique for improving performance in scalable systems. By storing frequently accessed data in memory, systems can reduce the need to repeatedly query databases or recalculate values. This is especially important for large-scale applications that handle millions of requests per second. Content delivery networks (CDNs) are a common caching solution for distributing static assets like images, videos, and scripts. CDNs store copies of content in multiple geographic locations, allowing users to access data from a server that is physically closer to them, reducing latency. Redis and Memcached are popular in-memory caching solutions that can store frequently accessed data, reducing the load on backend databases and improving system responsiveness.

The Human Side of Scalability: Organizational Challenges

Scaling a system is not just a technical challenge, it also presents significant organizational challenges. As a system grows, so too does the complexity of managing it, requiring larger teams, more specialized roles, and better communication between stakeholders.

1. Cross-Functional Collaboration: As discussed in previous chapters, engineering teams must collaborate closely with other departments, including product management, operations, and customer support, to ensure that scalability goals are aligned with business objectives. For example, engineers building a scalable payment processing system for a global e-commerce company need input from finance teams to understand compliance requirements in different countries, as well as from product teams to prioritize features. Cross-functional collaboration is essential for identifying bottlenecks and planning for future growth. Regular communication between teams ensures that engineers can proactively design systems to handle expected increases in traffic or new features that will demand additional resources.

2. DevOps and Automation: As systems scale, manual processes for deployment, monitoring, and maintenance become untenable. Engineers must adopt DevOps practices that emphasize automation, continuous integration, and continuous delivery (CI/CD). By automating deployment pipelines and using infrastructure-as-code tools like Terraform or Kubernetes, engineers can deploy updates more frequently and reliably at scale. Automation also plays a key role in monitoring system performance. Observability tools like Prometheus, Grafana, and Datadog allow engineers to track key metrics (such as CPU usage, memory consumption, and request latency) across distributed systems, ensuring that issues are detected and addressed before they impact users.

3. Scaling Engineering Teams: As systems scale, so do the teams that manage them. However, scaling engineering teams presents their own set of challenges. Larger teams require more coordination, more communication, and clearer roles and responsibilities. One of the key challenges for engineering leaders is maintaining productivity and agility as teams grow. Team autonomy is one solution to this challenge. By organizing teams around specific microservices or system components, companies can create smaller, independent teams that can operate with minimal dependencies on other teams. This allows for faster decision-making and reduces the complexity of managing large projects. Spotify is known for using this approach, organizing its engineering teams into "squads" that have the autonomy to manage their own services.

Scaling at Netflix

Netflix is one of the most iconic examples of a company that has successfully scaled its digital infrastructure to serve a global audience. With more than 200 million subscribers across the globe, Netflix must deliver high-quality video streaming services, often simultaneously, to millions of users in different regions and on different devices. To achieve this, Netflix has embraced many of the scalability principles discussed in this chapter. It uses a microservices architecture that allows different components of its platform (e.g., user profiles, recommendation algorithms, payment processing) to scale independently. This architecture ensures that if one component of the system experiences issues, the rest of the platform remains unaffected. Netflix also heavily relies on content delivery networks (CDNs) to ensure that its video content is delivered quickly and reliably to users around the world. By catching content in servers located near users, Netflix minimizes buffering and delivers a seamless viewing experience, even in regions with slower internet speeds.

Additionally, Netflix uses sophisticated load balancing and auto-scaling technologies to ensure that its platform can handle traffic spikes during popular show releases. Its infrastructure can dynamically allocate resources based on demand, ensuring that users experience minimal disruption even during periods of peak traffic. The success of Netflix's scaling efforts demonstrates the importance of building systems that are both flexible and resilient, capable of growing to meet global demand while maintaining a high level of performance. As the digital world continues to grow, the need for scalable, resilient systems will only increase. Engineers will be at the forefront of this effort, tasked with building the infrastructure that powers everything from global commerce to healthcare to entertainment. The challenges of scaling are significant, but by adopting best practices in architecture, automation, and collaboration, engineers can build systems that meet the needs of millions—if not billions—of users. In the next chapter, we will explore the role of engineers as innovators, driving disruption and change in industries around the world. But as we move forward, it's important to remember that the ability to scale is one of the defining characteristics of successful digital systems, and engineers must master the art of scaling to thrive in the digital age.

CHAPTER 5

Engineers as Innovators: Driving Disruption and Change

In today's fast-paced world, innovation is the currency of success. The most successful companies and industries are those that embrace change, disrupt existing norms, and continuously push the boundaries of what's possible. Engineers are at the heart of this innovation, playing a critical role in driving technological breakthroughs that reshape industries, create new markets, and transform how we live and work. While engineers have always been problem solvers, their role has evolved to that of innovators—creators of entirely new solutions that were once thought impossible. From the early days of the internet to the rise of artificial intelligence and autonomous vehicles, engineers have been the architects of change, building the systems that power the world's most disruptive technologies. This chapter will explore how engineers are driving innovation in industries across the globe, the mindset required to foster creativity and disruption, and the strategies that allow engineers to create lasting impact. We will examine case studies from industry leaders like Tesla, SpaceX, and Apple, highlighting how these companies have leveraged engineering talent to revolutionize their industries. We will also look at how engineers can cultivate a culture of innovation in their teams and organizations.

The Engineer's Role in Innovation

Innovation in technology isn't just about creating something new, it's about creating something better, faster, more efficient, or more accessible than what came before. Engineers are uniquely positioned to drive innovation because they have the technical expertise to turn bold ideas into reality. Whether it's improving an existing process or developing a completely new technology, engineers are often the ones who transform concepts into products, systems, or platforms that can scale and deliver value. At its core, innovation is about solving problems in new ways. For engineers, this often means looking beyond the immediate problem and considering the broader context in which their solution will be used. For example, the development of cloud computing wasn't just about making servers more efficient, it was about creating a scalable infrastructure that could power the future of the internet. Similarly, the development of the iPhone wasn't just about building a better phone, it was about reimagining how people interact with technology. **Disruptive innovation** occurs when engineers develop new technologies or systems that completely change the rules of the game. Often, this involves challenging long-held assumptions about how things are done, finding inefficiencies in existing processes, and applying new tools or methods to create something revolutionary. Engineers are at the forefront of such disruptions, leveraging new technologies like AI, machine learning, and quantum computing to create breakthroughs in industries ranging from healthcare to transportation.

Engineering Disruption: Key Characteristics

While not every engineer will work for a company like Tesla or Google, the principles of innovation and disruption are universal. Engineers who aspire to drive change need to embrace certain key characteristics that foster creativity and bold thinking. Below are some of the critical traits of engineers who excel as innovators:

1. Curiosity and Lifelong Learning: Innovation often begins with curiosity, the desire to understand how things work and how they can be improved. Engineers who question the status quo, explore new ideas, and continually seek to learn are better positioned to identify opportunities for innovation. This mindset of curiosity encourages engineers to explore new fields, experiment with emerging technologies, and stay ahead of industry trends. The rapid pace of technological change requires engineers to be lifelong learners. Keeping up with advancements in AI, blockchain, cybersecurity, and other areas requires engineers to constantly update their skills. Whether through formal education, self-study, or participating in industry conferences and hackathons, engineers who are committed to learning will be better equipped to drive innovation.

2. Risk-Taking and Embracing Failure: Innovation inherently involves risk. Engineers working on cutting-edge projects often face uncertain outcomes, and many experiments will fail before success is achieved. Innovators are those who embrace failure as a natural part of the process, learning from setbacks and using them as steppingstones toward eventual breakthroughs. Consider SpaceX, where failure has been a key part of the company's innovation process. The company's early rocket launches were met with several high-profile failures, including explosions and missed targets. However, rather than seeing these failures as the end of the road, engineers at SpaceX used them as learning opportunities, iterating on designs and eventually achieving historic successes such as the first private spacecraft to dock with the International Space Station. The willingness to take risks and embrace failure allows engineers to push the boundaries of what is possible, leading to innovations that would never be achieved if risk aversion were the dominant mindset.

3. Collaborative Problem-Solving: Innovation is rarely the work of a single person. Most breakthrough technologies are the result of collaboration between engineers, designers, business leaders, and other stakeholders. Engineers who excel as innovators are those who work effectively in teams, combining their technical expertise with insights from other disciplines to develop holistic solutions. Cross-functional collaboration is particularly important when it comes to innovation. Engineers must be able to work alongside product managers, data scientists, marketing teams, and other departments to ensure that their innovations are aligned with broader business goals and user needs. The most successful engineers understand that innovation is about solving real-world problems, and this requires input from a diverse set of perspectives. For example, in the development of the Apple Watch, engineers worked closely with designers to create a product that was not only technically advanced but also aesthetically pleasing and easy to use. This cross-disciplinary collaboration allowed Apple to create a product that appealed to a wide range of consumers and became a commercial success.

4. Focus on User Experience: One of the hallmarks of disruptive technologies is that they improve the user experience in ways that were previously unimagined. Engineers who focus on the end user—whether it's a consumer, a business, or an enterprise—are more likely to develop products that resonate with their target audience. This requires a deep understanding of user needs, preferences, and pain points. Engineers can drive innovation by thinking about how their solutions will be used in the real world and designing systems that are intuitive, user-friendly, and accessible. In the early days of software development, user experience was often an afterthought. Today, however, it is one of the key drivers of innovation, particularly in consumer-facing products. Design thinking is an approach that many engineers and innovators use to keep user experience at the forefront of the development process. This method involves empathizing with users, defining the problem, ideating potential solutions, prototyping, and testing. By focusing on the needs and experiences of users, engineers can create products that not only work well but also deliver exceptional value and satisfaction.

Tesla and the Disruption of the Automotive Industry

One of the most iconic examples of engineering-driven innovation is Tesla, the company that revolutionized the automotive industry by proving that electric vehicles (EVs) could be both desirable and commercially viable. Prior to Tesla's rise, electric vehicles were often dismissed as impractical, with limited range, high costs, and poor performance compared to traditional gasoline-powered cars. Tesla's engineers, led by CEO Elon Musk, took a different approach. Rather than seeing EVs as a niche market, Tesla envisioned a future where electric vehicles would dominate the automotive industry. Tesla's engineering team focused on solving the key technical challenges that had historically held back EVs, including battery efficiency, range, and performance. Tesla's Model S, released in 2012, was a turning point. It demonstrated that electric cars could be fast, stylish, and capable of long-range driving, effectively dispelling the myths surrounding EV limitations. The innovation didn't stop at the car itself—Tesla's engineers also developed the company's Supercharger network, enabling drivers to charge their cars quickly and efficiently across long distances, addressing one of the biggest concerns about electric vehicle adoption. The impact of Tesla's innovation has been profound. The success of Tesla's vehicles has spurred other automakers to invest heavily in electric vehicles, leading to a global shift toward cleaner, more sustainable transportation. Tesla's engineering innovations didn't just improve cars, they disrupted an entire industry.

Cultivating a Culture of Innovation in Engineering Teams

While some innovations come from individual genius, most are the result of a supportive culture that fosters creativity and experimentation. For engineers to drive innovation within their teams and organizations, certain cultural factors need to be in place. Below are some of the strategies that companies can use to cultivate a culture of innovation:

1. Encourage Experimentation Innovation requires experimentation, and experimentation often means trying things that might not work. Companies that encourage engineers to experiment—without fear of failure—are more likely to see breakthrough innovations. This requires creating an environment where engineers feel comfortable taking risks and proposing bold ideas, even if they don't always pan out. Google's "20% time" is a famous example of a company encouraging experimentation. Engineers at Google are allowed to spend 20% of their time working on side projects that aren't necessarily related to their core responsibilities. This policy has led to the development of some of Google's most successful products, including Gmail and Google News.

2. Reward Creativity Recognizing and rewarding creative solutions is another way to foster innovation within engineering teams. This doesn't mean only celebrating big breakthroughs, small improvements and creative problem-solving should also be acknowledged. When engineers see that their innovative thinking is valued, they are more likely to continue pursuing bold ideas.

3. Provide Resources: and Time for Innovation Engineers need both time and resources to innovate. Companies that prioritize short-term deliverables at the expense of long-term innovation often miss out on the next big idea. Providing engineers with dedicated time to work on innovative projects, as well as access to the tools and technologies they need, is essential for fostering a culture of innovation.

4. Promote Diversity of Thought: Diversity of thought is a key driver of innovation. Teams made up of individuals with diverse backgrounds, perspectives, and experiences are more likely to generate creative solutions to complex problems. Promoting inclusivity and encouraging engineers to collaborate across disciplines and departments can lead to more innovative outcomes.

The Future of Engineering-Driven Innovation

As we look ahead, the role of engineers in driving innovation will only become more important. Emerging technologies like quantum computing, blockchain, biotechnology, and renewable energy are poised to disrupt entire industries in ways that we can only begin to imagine. Engineers will be at the forefront of these disruptions, tasked with building the systems that power the future. But the future of innovation isn't just about new technologies, it's also about how engineers approach problem-solving, collaboration, and creativity. Engineers who embrace a mindset of curiosity, risk-taking, and collaboration will be best positioned to drive the next wave of breakthroughs that will shape the world. Engineers are more than just problem solvers—they are agents of change, driving innovation and disruption in industries across the globe. By embracing creativity, collaboration, and bold thinking, engineers can develop the technologies that will define the future. From electric vehicles to cloud computing to artificial intelligence, the work of engineers has the power to transform the world, and the opportunities for innovation have never been greater. In the next chapter, we will explore the impact of artificial intelligence and automation on the future of coding, examining how these technologies are transforming the role of engineers and shaping the future of software development. But as we move forward, it's important to remember that innovation is not just about technology, it's about the people and processes that make breakthroughs possible.

CHAPTER 6

The Future of Coding: AI, Automation, and Beyond

The world of software development is on the cusp of a major transformation, driven by the rise of artificial intelligence (AI) and automation. What once required intricate human intervention and hands-on coding is increasingly being streamlined, automated, and enhanced by powerful machine learning algorithms, AI-driven development tools, and automated processes. As these technologies evolve, they are reshaping the role of the engineer, fundamentally altering the way software is designed, built, and deployed. In this chapter, we explore the future of coding, focusing on the impact of AI, automation, and emerging technologies on software development. We will discuss how these innovations are changing the engineering landscape, the new skills engineers must develop to stay relevant, and how AI-driven tools can enhance productivity, creativity, and problem-solving. We will also consider the ethical and societal implications of increased automation in coding and the evolving relationship between engineers and the machines they build.

The Role of AI in Software Development

Artificial intelligence has made significant strides in recent years, moving from the realm of theoretical research into practical applications that affect nearly every industry. In the world of software development, AI is playing an increasingly important role, automating tasks, improving efficiency, and even generating code.

1. AI-Driven Code Generation: One of the most significant developments in AI's role in coding is the ability to generate code automatically. AI tools like GitHub Copilot, powered by OpenAI's GPT models, can now assist developers by suggesting code snippets, completing functions, and automating repetitive coding tasks. These AI-driven code assistants work alongside engineers, speeding up the development process by generating boilerplate code or recommending solutions based on vast databases of pre-existing code. For example, a developer working on a web application might use GitHub Copilot to suggest a common login authentication pattern, complete with validation and security best practices. Instead of writing this from scratch, the engineer can focus on customizing and refining the logic specific to the application. While these tools are not yet a replacement for human developers, they have the potential to significantly reduce the amount of time spent on routine tasks, allowing engineers to focus on more complex and creative aspects of development. As AI-powered tools become more sophisticated, they will likely take on more responsibility for writing code, with human engineers focusing on overseeing, refining, and guiding the process.

2. AI in Testing and Debugging: AI is also transforming the way engineers approach testing and debugging. Traditionally, testing has been one of the most time-consuming and tedious parts of software development, requiring engineers to manually create test cases, run tests, and track down bugs. AI-powered testing tools can now automate much of this process, generating test cases, running simulations, and identifying bugs with minimal human intervention. For example, tools like Testim and Mabl use machine learning to automatically generate and execute test scripts based on user interactions with an application. These tools can adapt to changes in the codebase, identifying regressions and potential issues that might be missed by human testers. In addition, AI-driven debugging tools help engineers identify the root causes of bugs more quickly. DeepCode, for example, uses machine learning to scan codebases for potential errors, security vulnerabilities, and inefficiencies, offering recommendations on how to fix them. These tools can significantly speed up the debugging process, allowing engineers to spend more time on innovation and less time tracking down bugs.

3. AI for Optimization and Performance Tuning: Another area where AI is making an impact is in optimizing software performance. Machine learning algorithms can analyze vast amounts of data to identify bottlenecks, optimize resource allocation, and improve overall system efficiency. For example, AI-driven tools can automatically adjust memory usage, optimize database queries, and recommend architectural changes to improve the scalability and performance of an application. Engineers at companies like Google and Amazon are already using AI to optimize their massive cloud infrastructures, ensuring that resources are allocated efficiently and that systems can scale seamlessly to handle millions of users. In addition, AI can be used to monitor live systems, detecting performance issues in real time and automatically making adjustments to maintain optimal performance.

Automation in Software Development: DevOps and CI/CD

While AI is making significant strides in code generation, testing, and optimization, automation has already been transforming the software development landscape through DevOps practices and Continuous Integration/Continuous Delivery (CI/CD) pipelines. These practices focus on automating the deployment, testing, and monitoring of software, ensuring that code can be delivered quickly and reliably to production environments.

1. Continuous Integration and Continuous Delivery (CI/CD) In the past, software development often followed a linear process, with code being written, tested, and deployed in large, infrequent releases. This model led to long development cycles, delayed feedback, and increased risks of bugs and errors in

production. CI/CD pipelines, powered by automation tools, have revolutionized this process, enabling engineers to continuously integrate and deploy small code changes, often multiple times a day. CI/CD pipelines automate the process of building, testing, and deploying code, reducing the need for manual intervention. Engineers can push code to a repository, and automated systems will compile the code, run tests, and deploy the application to a staging or production environment. This approach significantly reduces the time between writing code and delivering it to users, allowing for faster feedback loops and more agile development practices. Tools like Jenkins, CircleCI, and GitLab CI are widely used in the industry to automate CI/CD pipelines. These tools help engineers maintain high-quality code by running tests and checks automatically before deploying changes, ensuring that new features or updates don't introduce bugs or break existing functionality.

2. Infrastructure as Code (IaC): Another key aspect of automation in software development is the concept of Infrastructure as Code (IaC). IaC allows engineers to define and manage infrastructure (servers, databases, networks, etc.) using code, enabling them to automate the provisioning and configuration of resources. Tools like Terraform and Ansible allow engineers to write scripts that define how their infrastructure should be set up and managed. These scripts can then be run automatically to provision cloud resources, configure servers, and set up networking, all without manual intervention. IaC has become essential for managing complex, scalable systems in cloud environments, enabling rapid deployment and reducing the risk of configuration errors. By automating infrastructure management, engineers can focus on developing and deploying software, knowing that their infrastructure will be set up consistently and reliably across environments.

The Evolving Role of Engineers in the Age of AI and Automation

As AI and automation take over many of the routine tasks traditionally performed by engineers, the role of the modern software engineer is evolving. Rather than spending most of their time writing boilerplate code or configuring infrastructure, engineers are increasingly focusing on higher-level tasks such as system design, architecture, and problem-solving. However, this shift requires engineers to develop new skills and embrace new ways of working.

1. Architecting Intelligent Systems: as AI becomes more integrated into software systems, engineers will need to focus on designing and architecting intelligent systems that can operate autonomously and adapt to changing conditions. This involves designing systems that leverage machine learning algorithms, data pipelines, and AI models to automate decision-making and optimize performance. Engineers will also need to ensure that these systems are scalable, secure, and explainable. As AI systems become more complex, understanding how they make decisions and ensuring that they are free from bias or unintended consequences will be critical. Engineers will play a key role in building AI systems that are transparent, accountable, and aligned with ethical standards.

2. Collaboration with AI Tools: The relationship between engineers and AI will increasingly resemble a collaboration, where AI tools assist engineers in solving problems, generating code, and optimizing systems. Rather than replacing engineers, AI will serve as a powerful assistant, augmenting their capabilities and allowing them to work more efficiently. Engineers who embrace AI tools will be able to focus on creative problem-solving and innovation, using AI to handle the repetitive or tedious tasks that would otherwise slow them down. This shift will require engineers to develop a new mindset, one that is open to collaboration with AI and recognizes the value that these tools can bring to the development process.

3. The Rise of AI Literacy: as AI plays a greater role in software development, engineers will need to develop a deeper understanding of how AI works, including its strengths, limitations, and ethical implications. This will require engineers to develop AI literacy, the ability to understand, implement, and work with AI algorithms and systems. Engineers will need to learn new skills related to machine learning, data science, and AI model deployment. This includes understanding how to train and fine-tune machine learning models, how to integrate AI into existing systems, and how to ensure that AI-driven solutions are explainable and ethical. In addition, engineers will need to stay informed about the rapidly evolving landscape of AI technologies, including emerging frameworks, tools, and best practices.

Ethical and Societal Implications of AI and Automation in Coding

While AI and automation offer significant benefits for software development, they also raise important ethical and societal questions. As more of the coding process becomes automated, engineers must consider the long-term implications of these technologies and ensure that they are used responsibly.

1. Job Displacement and the Future of Work: One of the most significant concerns surrounding automation in software development is the potential for job displacement. As AI-driven tools take over more routine coding tasks, there is a risk that some engineering jobs could become obsolete, particularly those focused on lower-level tasks. However, rather than eliminating jobs, AI and automation are more likely to change the nature of engineering work. Engineers will increasingly focus on higher-level tasks such as system design, architecture, and strategic decision-making. To thrive in this new environment, engineers must continuously update their skills and embrace a mindset of lifelong learning.

2. Bias and Fairness in AI-Generated Code: AI systems are only as good as the data they are trained on, and biased data can lead to biased outcomes. As AI tools generate code and make decisions, engineers must ensure that these systems are free from bias and that the code they produce is fair, transparent, and inclusive. Engineers will play a critical role in auditing AI-driven tools, identifying potential biases in the data or algorithms, and ensuring that AI-generated solutions are ethical and responsible. This will require engineers to develop a deep understanding of the ethical implications of AI and to advocate for fairness and accountability in AI-driven systems.

The Future of Software Engineering in a Post-AI World

The rise of AI and automation represents a fundamental shift in the world of software engineering. While these technologies will undoubtedly change the way engineers work, they also present significant opportunities for innovation, creativity, and growth. By embracing AI-driven tools and automation, engineers can focus on solving the most complex and impactful problems, building the next generation of intelligent systems that will shape the future. As we move forward, engineers must be prepared to adapt to a world where AI plays an increasingly central role in software development. This will require a commitment to learning, collaboration, and ethical responsibility. The future of coding is bright, and engineers who embrace these changes will be at the forefront of technological innovation. The future of software development is being shaped by AI, automation, and emerging technologies that are transforming how engineers work. While these innovations bring significant benefits in terms of efficiency, productivity, and scalability, they also require engineers to adapt and develop new skills. Engineers who embrace AI as a collaborator, who understand the ethical implications of automation, and who are committed to continuous learning will thrive in this new landscape. In the next chapter, we will explore how engineers are tackling some of the world's most pressing challenges, including climate change and sustainability, by developing technologies that can help save the planet. As we move forward, the role of engineers will continue to expand, with AI and automation playing a central role in shaping the future of technology and society.

CHAPTER 7

Engineering for Sustainability: Coding to Save the Planet

In the 21st century, humanity faces some of its greatest challenges yet—chief among them is the growing threat of climate change. As the world becomes more interconnected and dependent on digital technologies, engineers have a unique opportunity and responsibility to contribute to solving the global sustainability crisis. From energy-efficient algorithms to technologies that help mitigate environmental damage, engineers can leverage their skills to build systems and solutions that not only drive innovation but also reduce the environmental footprint of human activities. This chapter explores how engineers are working to build a more sustainable future. We will discuss the principles of sustainable engineering, the development of green technologies, and the role of software in driving sustainability initiatives. Additionally, we will look at case studies from industries such as renewable energy, cloud computing, and transportation to illustrate how engineers are making a tangible difference in the fight against climate change.

The Role of Engineers in Addressing Climate Change

The tech industry has an outsized impact on the environment, contributing to carbon emissions, energy consumption, and e-waste. Data centers, which power the internet, consume vast amounts of electricity, while the manufacture of electronic devices results in significant resource extraction and waste. However, engineers are increasingly aware of these issues and are working on innovative ways to reduce the environmental impact of technology. At the same time, engineers are developing tools that help other industries become more sustainable. By creating software and systems that optimize energy use, reduce waste, and improve resource efficiency, engineers can make a significant contribution to global sustainability efforts. Sustainable engineering involves designing systems, processes, and products that minimize environmental impact, conserve resources, and promote long-term ecological balance. Engineers working in sustainability must think beyond immediate technical solutions and consider the broader impact of their work on the environment and society.

Principles of Sustainable Software Engineering

Sustainable software engineering goes beyond optimizing performance or writing efficient code—it involves designing software with the planet in mind. Below are some of the key principles that guide sustainable engineering efforts:

1. Energy Efficiency: One of the primary concerns in sustainable engineering is energy consumption. Digital systems, particularly cloud computing platforms, consume enormous amounts of energy to power servers, cool data centers, and process information. Engineers must prioritize energy efficiency when designing software and systems to reduce the overall carbon footprint of their technologies. This involves optimizing algorithms to reduce computational complexity, minimizing unnecessary data transfers, and ensuring that systems can operate at maximum efficiency with minimal energy consumption. For example, Google has developed AI-driven tools that optimize the energy usage of its data centers, reducing energy consumption for cooling by 30% and leading to significant reductions in carbon emissions.

2. Resource Conservation: Engineers can play a key role in conserving resources by designing systems that use less hardware and by building software that extends the lifespan of electronic devices. Software that reduces the strain on hardware components, such as power-efficient operating systems or applications that minimize CPU and memory usage, can help extend the life of devices, reducing e-waste. In addition, cloud-based solutions that allow for shared infrastructure reduce the need for individual companies to maintain their own data centers. This reduces the total number of servers required globally, conserving resources and reducing the overall environmental impact of data storage.

3. Minimalism and Simplicity: Sustainable engineering embraces the idea of minimalism—building systems that are as simple as possible to achieve their goals without unnecessary complexity. Software systems that are bloated with extraneous features not only require more energy to run but also increase the burden on hardware resources. Engineers can contribute to sustainability by developing lightweight software that avoids feature bloat and focuses on core functionality. Minimalism also applies to code itself. Writing clean, concise, and efficient code can reduce the computational power required to execute a program. This is particularly important in high-traffic applications where even small inefficiencies can lead to significant increases in energy consumption when scaled across millions of users.

4. Circular Economy and Reusability: Another principle of sustainable engineering is the promotion of a circular economy—a system in which products and materials are reused, repaired, and recycled rather than discarded. Engineers can contribute to a circular economy by designing software that supports repairability and reusability, ensuring that devices and systems can be easily maintained and updated. Open-source software, for example, supports the idea of reusability by allowing engineers to build on existing code rather than creating new solutions from scratch. This reduces the need for redundant development and helps promote a culture of shared resources and collaboration in the tech industry.

Building Green Technologies

Engineers are at the forefront of developing new technologies that support sustainability. From renewable energy systems to smart cities and electric vehicles, engineers are designing innovative solutions that help reduce carbon emissions and promote environmentally friendly practices. Let's explore some of the key areas where engineering is driving sustainability:

1. Renewable Energy: Renewable energy technologies, such as solar, wind, and hydropower, are critical in reducing the world's reliance on fossil fuels. Engineers working in this field are developing more efficient solar panels, designing wind turbines that can generate power under a wider range of conditions, and optimizing energy storage systems to store excess energy from renewable sources for later use. Software plays a key role in managing and optimizing renewable energy systems. For example, energy management systems (EMS) use advanced algorithms to monitor energy generation and consumption in real time, ensuring that renewable energy is used as efficiently as possible. These systems help integrate renewable energy sources into the grid, balancing supply and demand and reducing the need for fossil-fuel-based backup power.

2. Smart Grids: Engineers are also developing smart grid technologies, which use digital communication tools to monitor and manage the distribution of electricity across the grid. Smart grids allow utilities to detect and respond to fluctuations in energy demand, improve energy efficiency, and integrate renewable energy sources more effectively. One of the key innovations in smart grids is the use of machine learning and predictive analytics to forecast energy demand and optimize the distribution of electricity. Engineers can use these tools to ensure that electricity is distributed in a way that minimizes energy waste and reduces the need for backup power from non-renewable sources.

3. Electric Vehicles and Sustainable Transportation: The transportation sector is one of the largest contributors to global carbon emissions, but engineers are working to change that by developing electric vehicles (EVs) and alternative modes of transportation. Companies like Tesla have led the way in building electric cars that offer performance, range, and convenience that rival traditional gasoline-powered vehicles. Engineers in the EV industry are working to improve battery efficiency, reduce charging times, and expand the infrastructure for electric vehicle charging stations. Software plays a critical role in managing the complex systems that power EVs, optimizing battery usage, and providing real-time data on vehicle performance. In addition to electric vehicles, engineers are developing autonomous transportation systems that could further reduce emissions by optimizing routes, reducing traffic congestion, and promoting ridesharing. These technologies have the potential to revolutionize urban transportation, making it more efficient, sustainable, and accessible.

Smart Cities and IoT for Sustainability: Smart cities use technology to improve the efficiency of urban infrastructure and reduce the environmental impact of cities. Engineers are developing systems that monitor and manage traffic, energy usage, waste management, and water distribution, all with the goal of reducing emissions and promoting sustainability. The Internet of Things (IoT) plays a critical role in smart city initiatives by enabling devices to communicate and share data in real time. For example, smart traffic lights can adjust signal timings based on real-time traffic conditions, reducing congestion and emissions. Engineers working on IoT technologies are developing low-power sensors, efficient communication protocols, and data analytics platforms that help cities optimize resource usage and reduce their carbon footprints.

Google's Quest for a Carbon-Free Future

One of the most high-profile examples of sustainability efforts in the tech industry is Google's commitment to achieving a carbon-free future. As one of the largest data center operators in the world, Google has long recognized the need to reduce its environmental impact and has invested heavily in renewable energy and sustainable technologies. In 2017, Google became the first major company to match 100% of its global electricity consumption with purchases of renewable energy. However, the company has gone even further, aiming to operate entirely on carbon-free energy 24/7 by 2030. Achieving this ambitious goal requires innovation across multiple engineering disciplines.

Google's engineers have developed AI-driven tools that optimize the energy usage of its data centers. These systems monitor temperature, humidity, and energy consumption in real time and make automatic adjustments to reduce cooling needs and energy usage. By using AI to continuously fine-tune its operations, Google has reduced its data center energy consumption by 30%, significantly lowering its carbon footprint. In addition to optimizing its own operations, Google is also investing in clean energy projects around the world, from solar farms to wind energy initiatives. These projects help expand the availability of renewable energy and support the company's goal of building a sustainable future for the planet. Google's efforts demonstrate how engineering innovation can drive sustainability in the tech industry. By leveraging AI, data analytics, and renewable energy, the company is not only reducing its own environmental impact but also setting an example for other tech companies to follow.

The Future of Sustainable Engineering

The need for sustainable engineering will only grow as the world confronts the challenges of climate change and resource scarcity. Engineers will continue to play a central role in developing the technologies that help reduce carbon emissions, conserve resources, and promote environmental stewardship. Emerging technologies such as quantum computing and next-generation energy storage offer new opportunities for engineers to contribute to sustainability. For example, quantum computing has the potential to revolutionize energy optimization by solving complex problems that are currently intractable with classical computers.

Engineers working in this field could develop algorithms that optimize everything from energy grids to supply chains, reducing waste and improving efficiency. In addition, the continued development of carbon capture and storage (CCS) technologies could play a key role in mitigating the effects of climate change. Engineers are working on systems that capture carbon dioxide from the atmosphere and store it underground, helping to reduce the amount of greenhouse gases in the atmosphere. Engineers will also need to continue addressing the ethical and societal implications of their work, ensuring that the technologies they develop promote sustainability and social equity. This includes considering the environmental impact of new technologies from the earliest stages of design and working to ensure that the benefits of green technologies are shared by all.

As the world grapples with the urgent need to address climate change, engineers have a unique opportunity to lead the way toward a more sustainable future. By applying the principles of sustainable engineering, developing green technologies, and optimizing digital systems for energy efficiency, engineers can help mitigate the environmental impact of human activities and build a world that is cleaner, greener, and more resilient. In the next chapter, we will explore the role of engineers in fostering collaboration and innovation across global, interdisciplinary teams. But as we move forward, it's important to remember that sustainability must be at the heart of all engineering efforts. Engineers have the power to save the planet—one line of code, one solution, and one system at a time.

CHAPTER 8

The Collaborative Engineer: Working in a Global, Interdisciplinary World

As technology continues to evolve at a rapid pace, the challenges engineers face have become more complex and interconnected. The days when engineers worked in isolation, focused solely on technical problems within their specialized domains, are long gone. Today, engineers must collaborate across disciplines, industries, and even national borders to solve problems that are global in scope and often require expertise from multiple fields. The modern engineer is a collaborator, working alongside product managers, designers, data scientists, marketers, and stakeholders from various disciplines. Collaboration has become essential not only for building complex software systems but also for driving innovation, managing large-scale projects, and ensuring that technological solutions align with business goals and user needs. This chapter will explore the importance of collaboration in engineering, the tools and practices that facilitate cross-functional teamwork, and the growing trend of global engineering teams working across time zones and borders.

The Importance of Collaboration in Engineering

Collaboration is at the heart of modern engineering because the problems engineers are tasked with solving are increasingly interdisciplinary and require diverse perspectives. Whether it's building a global-scale cloud infrastructure, developing a cutting-edge artificial intelligence (AI) algorithm, or designing a user-friendly mobile app, these projects often demand input from a range of experts. One of the primary reasons collaborations has become so essential in engineering is that systems have grown more complex and interconnected. Take the example of autonomous vehicles: engineers working on these systems must collaborate with data scientists to develop machine learning models, work with hardware engineers to ensure sensors and cameras are reliable and engage with policy experts to navigate legal and regulatory issues. No single engineer can master all of these areas, which makes teamwork and collaboration indispensable.

Key benefits of collaboration in engineering include:

1. Diverse Perspectives Lead to Better Solutions Bringing together people with different skills, backgrounds, and perspectives can lead to more innovative and effective solutions. In engineering, it's common to encounter problems that cannot be solved from a purely technical perspective. For example, developing a new software product requires not only technical expertise but also an understanding of user experience, business strategy, and market trends. By collaborating with designers, marketers, and business analysts, engineers can ensure that their solutions are well-rounded and address the needs of end-users.

2. Faster Problem-Solving: Cross-functional teams can often solve problems faster than individuals or siloed teams working in isolation. When engineers work closely with other departments, they can identify roadblocks early and address them collaboratively. For example, if an engineering team is working on a new feature for a software product, involving the product manager and customer support team early in the process can help avoid potential issues related to customer expectations or market fit.

3. Improved Communication and Alignment Collaboration ensures that all stakeholders are aligned on project goals, timelines, and deliverables. In large projects, miscommunication or misalignment between teams can lead to costly delays or failures. By fostering a culture of open communication and teamwork, engineers can ensure that all teams are on the same page, which improves overall project efficiency and outcomes.

Cross-Functional Teams: The New Normal

One of the most significant trends in engineering is the rise of cross-functional teams, where engineers work alongside professionals from other disciplines such as design, product management, marketing, and operations. In this model, engineers are not just focused on writing code or developing technical solutions; they also play a role in defining product features, ensuring user satisfaction, and aligning their work with business objectives. Cross-functional teams are typically organized around specific projects or products, and each team member contributes their expertise to achieve the team's shared goals. For example, in a software development project, a cross-functional team might consist of:

Software Engineers: Responsible for writing code, developing backend systems, and ensuring the technical feasibility of the project.

Product Managers: Focused on defining the project's goals, ensuring that it meets market needs, and aligning the team's work with business objectives.

Designers: Responsible for creating the user interface (UI) and user experience (UX) design, ensuring that the product is intuitive, visually appealing, and accessible.

Data Scientists: Analyzing user data and providing insights that inform product development, such as identifying usage patterns or predicting user behavior.

Operations/DevOps Engineers: Ensuring that the infrastructure can support the application's scalability and reliability, and automating deployment and monitoring processes.

Global Engineering Teams: Working Across Borders and Time Zones

In today's global economy, many engineering teams are distributed across different countries and time zones. This trend has been accelerated by the rise of remote work, which has enabled companies to tap into a global talent pool. Engineers are now working on projects with colleagues from different parts of the world, often overcoming language and cultural barriers to deliver world-class solutions.

Global engineering teams offer several advantages, including:

Access to Global Talent: By hiring engineers from different parts of the world, companies can access a broader pool of expertise and skills. This is particularly valuable for specialized fields such as artificial intelligence, machine learning, and cybersecurity, where talent shortages in one region can be offset by hiring from a global workforce.

Round-the-Clock Productivity: One of the key benefits of global teams is the ability to work around the clock. When engineers in one time zone finish their workday, engineers in another time zone can pick up where they left off, ensuring continuous progress on projects. This "follow-the-sun" model is particularly valuable for time-sensitive projects and companies that need to provide 24/7 support or services.

Diverse Perspectives and Innovation: Working with a globally diverse team brings a variety of perspectives and approaches to problem-solving. Engineers from different cultural backgrounds may have different ways of thinking about challenges, which can lead to more innovative and creative solutions. Global teams are also better equipped to build products that serve diverse user bases, as they are more likely to understand and incorporate the needs of users from different regions and cultures.

However, managing global engineering teams also comes with challenges, such as coordinating work across different time zones, ensuring clear communication, and maintaining a strong team culture despite the physical distance.

Tools and Practices for Effective Collaboration

Effective collaboration requires more than just a willingness to work together—it also depends on using the right tools and practices to ensure smooth communication, transparency, and coordination across teams. Engineers working in global and cross-functional teams rely on a range of tools to manage projects, share information, and track progress. Below are some of the key tools and practices that facilitate collaboration in modern engineering teams:

Communication Tools: Communication is the foundation of collaboration, and teams need robust tools to stay connected, especially when working remotely or across time zones. Tools like Slack, Microsoft Teams, and Zoom allow engineers to communicate in real time, share updates, and resolve issues quickly. In addition to real-time communication, asynchronous communication tools such as email or project management platforms like Trello and Asana allow team members to stay informed and collaborate even when they are not online at the same time.

Version Control and Code Collaboration: In software development, version control systems like Git and platforms like GitHub or GitLab are essential for collaborative coding. These tools allow engineers to work on the same codebase, track changes, and resolve conflicts when merging code. Engineers can also use pull requests and code reviews to collaborate on features and ensure that the quality of the code is maintained. For globally distributed teams, version control systems provide a single source of truth, ensuring that all team members have access to the latest code and can contribute to the project without stepping on each other's toes.

Agile and Scrum Methodologies Agile methodologies, such as Scrum and Kanban, have become the standard approach for managing collaborative software development projects. Agile emphasizes iterative development, continuous feedback, and close collaboration between engineers, product managers, and other stakeholders. Scrum teams work in short cycles known as sprints, where they plan, execute, and review work in regular intervals. This approach allows teams to stay aligned, adapt to changing requirements, and continuously improve their processes. Engineers use tools like Jira or Trello to track tasks, assign work, and ensure that the team is making steady progress toward its goals.

DevOps and Continuous Integration/Continuous Delivery (CI/CD) DevOps practices, which emphasize collaboration between development and operations teams, are essential for delivering software on a scale. Engineers working on large projects use CI/CD pipelines to automate testing, integration, and deployment, allowing teams to release new features and updates more frequently and with fewer errors. Tools like Jenkins, CircleCI, and Travis CI are commonly used to automate these processes, ensuring that code can be integrated and deployed efficiently across multiple teams and environments.

Overcoming Common Challenges in Collaboration

While collaboration offers significant benefits, it also comes with challenges. Miscommunication, misalignment of goals, and cultural differences can all create friction in cross-functional or global teams. Below are some of the most common challenges in engineering collaboration and strategies for overcoming them:

Time Zone Differences: For global teams, time zone differences can make it difficult to schedule meetings or collaborate in real time. One solution is to schedule regular check-ins at times that overlap across time zones, ensuring that all team members can participate. For asynchronous communication, teams can use detailed documentation and status updates to keep everyone informed, regardless of when they are working.

Cultural Differences: Cultural differences can sometimes lead to misunderstandings or different expectations about how work should be done. It's important for teams to foster a culture of respect and openness, encouraging team members to share their perspectives and work styles. Cross-cultural training and team-building exercises can also help bridge gaps and create a more cohesive team.

Misalignment of Goals: In cross-functional teams, different departments may have different priorities. Engineers may be focused on technical excellence, while product managers prioritize time-to-market and customer satisfaction. To overcome this challenge, it's essential to align shared goals at the beginning of a project and maintain open communication throughout the development process.

Keeping Teams Motivated: In distributed teams, maintaining a sense of camaraderie and team spirit can be challenging. Regular virtual team-building activities, celebrating milestones, and recognizing individual contributions can help keep teams motivated and engaged. It's also important for engineering leaders to provide clear guidance, support, and opportunities for professional growth to keep their teams invested in the project.

The Future of Collaboration in Engineering

As the world becomes more interconnected and global, collaboration will continue to be a key factor in engineering success. Advances in communication technologies, virtual reality, and collaboration tools will make it even easier for engineers to work together across borders, bringing together diverse teams to solve increasingly complex problems. The future of engineering will also see greater collaboration between humans and machines, as AI-driven tools take on more tasks and assist engineers in their work. Rather than replacing engineers, AI will serve as a collaborator, helping engineers automate routine tasks, optimize processes, and generate new insights. As we look to the future, the ability to collaborate effectively—across disciplines, industries, and geographies—will be one of the most important skills engineers can cultivate. By embracing collaboration, engineers can build stronger teams, drive innovation, and solve the world's most pressing challenges. Collaboration is at the heart of modern engineering. Whether working with colleagues from other departments or teaming up with engineers from around the world, the ability to collaborate effectively is essential for delivering innovative solutions and driving success in today's global economy. In the next chapter, we will explore how engineers are building their legacy, shaping the future of humanity through the technologies they create. But as we move forward, it's important to remember that no engineer can build the future alone. It is through collaboration—across disciplines, industries, and borders—that engineers will solve the challenges of tomorrow.

CHAPTER 9

The Engineer's Legacy: Coding the Future of Humanity

As we look to the future, one thing is clear: engineers will play a pivotal role in shaping the world of tomorrow. The systems and technologies they design today will have long-lasting effects on societies, economies, and the environment. Engineers are the architects of the future, and their work will define how humans live, interact, and solve problems for generations to come. This chapter explores the legacy engineers leave behind through the technologies they create and how their contributions will shape the future of humanity. We will discuss how the work of engineers transcends the immediate impact of products and systems, creating a lasting legacy that influences the very fabric of society. From the ethical responsibilities of designing fair and inclusive systems to the long-term impact of AI and automation, this chapter reflects on the ways engineers can ensure their work contributes positively to the world, building a future that is not only technologically advanced but also equitable, sustainable, and inclusive.

The Long-Term Impact of Engineering Decisions

Every day, engineers make decisions that affect not only the immediate functionality of a system but also its long-term implications. Whether they are writing code for a new mobile app, designing algorithms for autonomous vehicles, or developing new energy storage solutions, engineers are making choices that will reverberate far beyond the confines of the project at hand. Scalability, security, and sustainability are just a few of the factors engineers must consider when building systems designed to last. The code they write today will be used, modified, and built upon by future generations of engineers, which means that the quality, maintainability, and ethical considerations behind that code must stand the test of time. Engineers, therefore, have a responsibility not only to solve immediate technical problems but also to think about the broader implications of their work. One of the most critical aspects of this responsibility is sustainability. Engineers must design systems that minimize environmental impact, conserve resources, and promote long-term ecological balance. For example, engineers building data centers must consider how their designs will affect energy consumption decades into the future, while those developing software for consumer products must think about how to extend the lifespan of devices and reduce electronic waste. Beyond sustainability, engineers must also account for social impact. The systems they create often have wide-reaching effects on how people live and work. For instance, the rise of social media platforms has fundamentally changed how people communicate, share information, and interact. These platforms were designed by engineers, and the decisions they made—about algorithms, user experience, and data privacy—have shaped the social and political landscapes of the 21st century.

The Legacy of AI and Automation

The rise of artificial intelligence (AI) and automation represents one of the most significant technological shifts of our time. These technologies have the potential to transform industries, create new opportunities, and solve problems that were once considered unsolvable. However, they also raise profound questions about the future of work, the economy, and human society. Engineers working in AI and automation are building systems that could redefine entire industries, from healthcare to manufacturing to transportation. AI-powered diagnostic tools, for example, are already being used to identify diseases more accurately and efficiently than human doctors in some cases. Autonomous vehicles promise to revolutionize transportation, reducing traffic accidents and improving efficiency. In manufacturing, automated robots are streamlining production processes, increasing productivity, and lowering costs. However, with these advancements come concerns about job displacement and the future of work. Automation has the potential to eliminate many jobs, particularly those that involve repetitive tasks. Engineers must consider how their innovations will impact the workforce and what steps can be taken to ensure that the benefits of automation are distributed equitably. This might involve designing systems that complement human workers rather than replace them or advocating for policies that provide retraining and support for displaced workers. The legacy of AI and automation will also depend on how these technologies are governed. Engineers must work closely with policymakers, ethicists, and civil society organizations to ensure that AI systems are designed and deployed in ways that are fair, transparent, and accountable. This will involve establishing clear ethical guidelines for AI development, creating mechanisms for auditing AI systems, and ensuring that AI technologies are aligned with societal values.

Engineering for Social Good

Engineers have always been problem solvers, and some of the most impactful contributions engineers can make are those that address global challenges such as poverty, inequality, and access to essential services. Through the development of innovative technologies, engineers have the potential to improve the quality of life for millions of people around the world. One of the most powerful examples of engineering for social good is the development of clean water technologies. Engineers working in this field have developed systems that provide safe drinking water to communities that lack access to clean water, helping to prevent waterborne diseases and improve public health. Technologies like solar-powered water purification systems, desalination plants, and rainwater harvesting solutions have had a transformative impact on communities around the world. In addition to clean water, engineers are working to improve access to renewable energy in developing countries. Off-grid solar power systems, for example, provide electricity to rural communities that are not connected to the national grid. These systems allow people to power their homes, run businesses, and access essential services like healthcare and education. Engineers are also using technology to address education and healthcare disparities. Mobile apps that provide access to online learning resources are helping students in underserved areas gain access to high-quality education. Telemedicine platforms are enabling doctors to reach patients in remote regions, providing life-saving medical care where it would otherwise be unavailable. By focusing on projects that have a positive social impact, engineers can leave a legacy that extends far beyond the immediate success of a product or system. Through their work, engineers can contribute to a more just, equitable, and sustainable world.

The Legacy of the Internet

Perhaps one of the most significant legacies of engineering is the creation of the internet—a technology that has fundamentally reshaped how humans communicate, work, and access information. The engineers who built the internet could never have predicted its vast impact, from revolutionizing global commerce to enabling social movements and providing a platform for free speech. The development of the internet was a collaborative effort involving engineers from around the world, and it was guided by principles of openness, accessibility, and decentralization. These engineers envisioned a global network that would connect people and provide access to knowledge, and their vision has become a reality. However, the internet has also raised important ethical and social challenges. The rise of cybersecurity threats, privacy concerns, and misinformation has forced engineers to rethink how the internet is governed and how its negative impacts can be mitigated. Engineers working on the next phase of the internet, whether through advancements in blockchain, Web3, or other technologies—will need to ensure that the internet remains a force for good. The legacy of the internet shows that the work of engineers can have profound, far-reaching effects that extend beyond the original goals of the technology. Engineers working today have the opportunity to build systems that, like the internet, will shape the course of human history.

Building a Legacy: What Will Your Impact Be?

As an engineer, you are in a unique position to leave a lasting legacy. The systems, algorithms, and technologies you create will not only solve today's problems but also influence how future generations live and interact with the world. Whether you are developing cutting-edge AI systems, building sustainable technologies, or improving access to essential services, your work will have an impact that extends far beyond the present. To build a legacy that you can be proud of, it's important to focus not only on technical excellence but also on the ethical, social, and environmental implications of your work. Consider how your decisions will affect users, communities, and the planet in the long term. Strive to create technologies that empower people, promote equity, and protect the environment. Ultimately, the legacy of an engineer is not just measured by the products they create but by the positive impact they have on society. As you continue your journey as an engineer, remember that every line of code, every system, and every innovation is an opportunity to shape the future. What kind of future do you want to build? Engineers have the power to shape the future of humanity through the technologies they create. The systems built today will define the way we live, work, and interact for generations to come. Whether addressing climate change, promoting equity, or driving technological innovation, engineers have a responsibility to ensure that their work leaves a positive legacy. In the final chapter, we will reflect on how engineers can continue to lead in a rapidly changing world, embracing new technologies, collaborating across disciplines, and taking on the challenges of tomorrow. But as we conclude this chapter, remember that your legacy as an engineer is being built every day—with every decision, every system, and every line of code.

CHAPTER 10

Engineering with Purpose: Leading in a Rapidly Changing World

The world is changing at a faster pace than ever before. Technological breakthroughs in artificial intelligence, quantum computing, biotechnology, and renewable energy are reshaping industries and redefining the boundaries of what's possible. Engineers stand at the forefront of these transformations, equipped with the skills and knowledge to drive innovation and solve some of humanity's most pressing challenges. But with this incredible power comes responsibility. To thrive in this rapidly evolving landscape, engineers must not only be technically proficient but also lead with vision, purpose, and a sense of responsibility to society and the planet. This chapter reflects on the journey engineers have taken throughout this book and emphasizes the qualities, values, and practices that will help them succeed in the future. We'll explore how engineers can continue to lead and innovate in a world marked by constant change, uncertainty, and complexity. As engineers build the technologies of tomorrow, their work will not only shape industries but also have profound impacts on society, culture, and the environment. Engineering with purpose means creating solutions that are not only cutting-edge but also ethical, inclusive, and sustainable.

Engineering in a Time of Rapid Change

The digital revolution has ushered in an era of rapid technological progress, with new tools, platforms, and systems emerging at an unprecedented pace. This continuous wave of innovation has disrupted entire industries, transforming how businesses operate and how individuals engage with technology. For engineers, this environment of constant change presents both challenges and opportunities.

Embracing Technological Change: Engineers must continuously adapt to the evolving landscape of technology, learning new programming languages, frameworks, and methodologies as they emerge. Technologies such as artificial intelligence (AI), blockchain, cloud computing, and 5G have introduced new paradigms in software development, networking, and data management. To stay ahead, engineers must embrace a mindset of continuous learning and professional development. The rapid pace of change means that engineers must remain agile, ready to pivot when new technologies or practices emerge. This can be seen in the rise of cloud-native development, where engineers design applications specifically for cloud platforms, as opposed to the traditional on-premises models. Engineers who can anticipate and leverage these trends will be in the best position to drive innovation and stay competitive.

Solving Complex, Global Problems: Many of the challenges engineers face today are global in scope and complexity, from addressing climate change to ensuring cybersecurity in a hyperconnected world. The solutions to these problems require interdisciplinary collaboration and a deep understanding of both technology and the broader social and environmental contexts in which it operates. Engineers must learn to navigate the complexities of building systems that not only function well but also align with global sustainability goals, ethical standards, and human values. For example, designing energy-efficient data centers requires an understanding of both software optimization and environmental science, while building secure communication platforms necessitates collaboration between engineers, policymakers, and ethicists to protect privacy and prevent misuse.

Leading Innovation in Disruptive Times: As industries continue to be disrupted by digital transformation, engineers will be called upon to lead innovation and help organizations navigate change. Companies across sectors, from finance to healthcare to manufacturing, are increasingly relying on engineers to drive digital transformation initiatives, develop new products, and improve operational efficiency through automation and data analytics. Engineers must embrace leadership roles, guiding teams, setting technical direction, and fostering a culture of innovation within their organizations. Whether they are leading a development team or collaborating with business leaders, engineers must develop strong communication, project management, and strategic thinking skills to drive meaningful change.

Purpose-Driven Engineering

While technical excellence remains critical to success, engineers today must also lead with purpose. Purpose-driven engineering is about building solutions that have a positive impact on society, protect the environment, and promote inclusivity. It's about recognizing that every system engineer design, every algorithm they write, and every product they launch has the potential to shape the future for better or worse.

Engineering for Social Good: Engineers have the power to create technologies that improve lives and advance social good. Whether it's developing clean water technologies for underserved communities, creating affordable renewable energy solutions, or designing telemedicine platforms that extend healthcare access to rural areas, engineers are in a unique position to address global inequities and challenges. One of the growing trends in purpose-driven engineering is the development of tech for good initiatives. These projects focus on using technology to solve social problems, such as poverty, healthcare disparities, and access to education. By leveraging their skills for the betterment of society, engineers can leave a lasting positive legacy.

Sustainability as a Core Principle: Engineers must incorporate sustainability into every aspect of their work. From the design of energy-efficient algorithms to the development of green technologies, engineers have the potential to make a significant contribution to the fight against climate change. Sustainable engineering means not only reducing the environmental impact of digital systems but also creating solutions that promote long-term ecological balance. Companies like Tesla, Google, and Microsoft have demonstrated how engineers can drive sustainability initiatives by developing innovative technologies that reduce carbon emissions, optimize energy consumption, and promote the use of renewable energy sources. Engineers working in these fields are not only advancing technological progress but also helping create a more sustainable world for future generations.

Inclusivity and Diversity in Technology: Engineers have the opportunity to create technologies that are inclusive, accessible, and representative of diverse user needs. Ensuring that products and services are accessible to people of all abilities, backgrounds, and locations requires a commitment to inclusivity in both design and development processes. Inclusive engineering means considering how different groups of users will interact with a product and designing systems that are usable and beneficial for everyone. This includes accessibility features, language inclusivity, and designing for underserved markets. Engineers who prioritize inclusivity are helping build a more equitable and just world, where technology empowers all individuals, not just a select few.

Promoting Innovation Through Collaboration and Leadership

In this new era of engineering, collaboration and leadership are more important than ever. Engineers must work across disciplines, industries, and borders to solve the increasingly complex challenges of the digital age. At the same time, they must lead teams, projects, and organizations with a clear vision of how technology can be used to create positive change.

Leading Engineering Teams: Engineers who take on leadership roles have the opportunity to shape not only the direction of their projects but also the culture of their teams. Effective engineering leaders foster a culture of creativity, collaboration, and continuous improvement. They encourage experimentation, support professional growth, and ensure that their teams are aligned with both technical and business goals. Leadership in engineering also involves advocating for purpose-driven projects that prioritize sustainability, ethics, and inclusivity. Engineers who lead with purpose can inspire their teams to tackle the most pressing challenges of our time and create technologies that have a lasting positive impact on society.

Collaboration Across Disciplines: As discussed in previous chapters, collaboration across disciplines is essential for driving innovation and solving complex problems. Engineers must work closely with professionals from other fields—whether it's collaborating with designers to create user-friendly products or working with policymakers to develop regulations for emerging technologies. Engineers who can collaborate effectively across disciplines are better equipped to develop holistic solutions that address both technical and societal needs. For example, engineers working on autonomous vehicles must collaborate with ethicists, urban planners, and policymakers to ensure that their systems are safe, equitable, and aligned with public interests.

Global Collaboration and Remote Work: In today's interconnected world, engineers are increasingly working on global teams that span multiple time zones and regions. Global collaboration enables engineers to tap into diverse perspectives, share knowledge, and develop solutions that work across different cultural and geographic contexts. The rise of remote work has also expanded opportunities for engineers to collaborate with colleagues from around the world. While working in distributed teams presents challenges related to communication and coordination, it also offers opportunities for engineers to participate in innovative projects, no matter where they are located. Embracing global collaboration and mastering the tools that enable effective remote teamwork will be key to success in the future of engineering.

The Engineer's Responsibility to the Future

As engineers continue to push the boundaries of innovation, they must remain mindful of the legacy they are building for future generations. The technologies created today will shape the world for decades to come, influencing how people live, work, and interact with each other. Engineers have a responsibility to ensure that the systems they build promote sustainability, equity, and human well-being. The future of humanity will be defined in part by the choices engineers make today—whether it's developing AI systems that respect privacy, creating sustainable energy solutions, or designing technologies that empower individuals rather than exploit them. Engineers are in a unique position to shape the future, and with that power comes the responsibility to build systems that contribute to a better world. As we come to the conclusion of this book, it's clear that engineers have an extraordinary role to play in shaping the future. The technologies they create will define the next chapter of human history, influencing how we address global challenges, interact with technology, and build a more equitable and sustainable world. To succeed in this rapidly changing world, engineers must lead with purpose, embracing their responsibility to society and the planet. By focusing on innovation, collaboration, sustainability, and ethics, engineers can build systems that not only solve today's problems but also create a brighter future for generations to come. As you continue your journey as an engineer, remember that every line of code, every system design, and every decision you make has the potential to shape the world. Lead with purpose, embrace change, and strive to build technologies that make a positive impact. The future is in your hands.

www.ingramcontent.com/pod-product-compliance
Ingram Content Group UK Ltd.
Pitfield, Milton Keynes, MK11 3LW, UK
UKHW042017290726
14061UKWH00001BB/43

9 789700 192857